Instagram Marketing in 2019 Made (Stupidly) Easy

Vol.5 of the Small Business Marketing Made (Stupidly) Easy Collection

by Michael Clarke

Founder, Punk Rock Marketing

Published in USA by: Punk Rock Marketing

Michael Clarke

© Copyright 2018

ISBN-13: 978-1-970119-14-5

Table of Contents

Chapter 2: Six Steps to a Profitable Instagram Profile 39

Chapter 5: The Perfect Instagram Post Checklist 84

Chapter 6: How to Create a Rabid Tribe of Zombie Instagram Followers 100

Chapter 7: Five Ninja-Hack Tools & Apps That Will Make You Money 116

Epilogue: "Toto, I Don't Think We're in Kansas Anymore" 131

About the Author

Michael Clarke is a former cubicle monkey turned social media marketing consultant and author. He is also the owner of the world's most neurotic Jack Russell Terrier.

Also By Michael Clarke

TWITTER MARKETING IN 2019 MADE
(STUPIDLY) EASY

VIDEO MARKETING IN 2019 MADE
STUPIDLY EASY

FACEBOOK MARKETING IN 2019 MADE
STUPIDLY EASY

PINTEREST MARKETING IN 2019 MADE
STUPIDLY EASY

LINKEDIN MARKETING IN 2019 MADE
STUPIDLY EASY

EMAIL MARKETING IN 2019 MADE
STUPIDLY EASY

SEARCH ENGINE OPTIMIZATION IN
2019 MADE STUPIDLY EASY

A Special FREE Gift for You!

If you'd like FREE instant access to my seminar "How to Make a Damn Good Living With Social Media (Even If You Hate Social Media" then head over to **PunkRockMarketing.com/Free.** (What else you gonna do? Watch another "Twilight" movie?!)

Prologue: Yeah, But How Do You Make Money With Instagram?

Unless you've been living under a Kardashian-free rock, you'll no doubt have heard Instagram is the NEW (gotta-use) marketing platform to reach ANYBODY under the age of 40.

The numbers are staggering, Instagram has nearly one billion monthly users. With year-over-year growth rates of nearly 200%. (Take that, Twitter.)

And there's a REASON Facebook paid 750 million dollars to acquire Instagram. They KNOW Facebook may be the perfect platform for Mom to connect with her book club. Or Dad to talk smack with his fellow Fantasy Football nerds. Or Grandma Jo to share some weird cat meme picture she found. ("Look, honey…the cat is playing a keyboard guitar!")

But the young, 18-35 demographic eyeballs — who have tons of discretionary income — are ALL on Instagram.

Big question for us marketers is how we get noticed in a sea of mirror selfies and shaky 15-second nightclub videos. (#DontThesePeopleHaveAJob)

Well, getting noticed, introducing these folks to our brand — and eventually getting them to give us their hard-earned (or sometimes hardly earned) Millennial cash is what this book is all about.

But before we jump into the trenches of Instagram marketing, before we dig into creating content and building a tribe of rabid Instagram followers, let me tell you the #1 way NOT to market to folks on Instagram.

And that is…

Sell.

Much ink has been spilled trying to "figure out" the consuming habits and core values of the "Millennial."

But one thing that's abundantly clear from all the research is folks aged 18-40 DON'T trust institutions or anything that smells "corporate."

It's as if they see life like some "Hunger Games" scenario where reality is a struggle over scarce resources, such as a full-time job or a free burrito at Chipotle. (While the corrupt adults who run companies sit back and watch.)

And if you intend to barge into Instagram with a formal, corporate "Go here and buy this thing" attitude then let me save you the time. It won't work.

Try Google AdWords. Or a Goodyear Blimp.

But if you're willing to show a hipper, more irreverent side of your business...

If you're willing to spend time "liking" and "commenting" on your tribe's posts...(nothing these folks love more than approval)

If you're able to connect your product or service with an aspirational lifestyle that makes Millennials look smart, beautiful and morally superior to the world (and that includes OTHER Millennials)...

...then you'll crush it on Instagram.

Still not convinced?

Don't worry if you can't quite see HOW it's all going to come together. I'm not gonna ask you to delve into complex HTML or spend hours a day "liking" and "commenting" on Instagram accounts.

I won't even ask you to take any selfie shots of your six-pack abs. (Or in my case twelve-pack abs.)

But I will encourage you to put your impulse to "sell" and "convert" on the back burner as you:

- Step #1 - Post stuff on Instagram that doesn't suck (which gets you followers and fans)
- Step #2 - Which leads to followers and fans clicking on the link in your Instagram bio that sends them to your lead-capture page

- Step #3 - You make a crap load of money and invite me to your party in Aruba when Facebook acquires your company

The Instagram crowd has a very refined radar for detecting B.S. marketing messages. But if you can get past the radar — in this book I'll show you how to do that — then not only will you find a ton of leads (and future customers) on Instagram.

But you'll find a motivated (and highly connected) army of young people who'll share your message...for FREE!

And that makes enduring a nightclub video or two worth it.

So, if you're ready to grab your crossbow...let the "Instagram Hunger Games" begin!

Introduction:

Newbie's Guide to Instagram

FAQ

"Thorough preparation makes its own luck."

-Joe Poyer

If you're an Instagram expert already — if you spend 11 hours each day finding the "perfect" sepia filter for your Instagram posts — then move on to Chapter 1. (You already KNOW everything I'm gonna cover here.)

But for those who have no clue how this popular, if strange, network works — or why people under 40 spend so much damn time on it...

…here are 5 Instagram FAQs to help guide you through the Instagram marketing process (and make you appear way smarter and hipper than you actually are.)

Instagram FAQ #1: What the Hell is Instagram? (And Why Is It So Damn Popular?)

Instagram is a photo-sharing social network that allows users to post photos to their profile — then tweak those photos with old-timey picture filters — which lets them share those pictures with their friends. (And with over 400 million monthly Instagram users, there's a lot of friends out there.)

As for WHY is it so popular, there are THREE key reasons:

1) **The lo-fi photo filters are cool.** These are the optional filters users can employ to give even the most ordinary photos drama and intensity. (Not to mention make everybody

look like a way better photographer than they actually are.)

2) **Instagram makes it easy to SHARE photos & videos with friends on the phone.** Unlike the mobile Twitter and Facebook app — which can take that extra 13 seconds to share a pic or video — Instagram is dead-easy to use from a user perspective.

3) **People use photos as their default "status update" increasingly.** This, my friends, is the WHOLE reason Facebook purchased Instagram. (It wasn't the filter technology.) They looked into their crystal ball and realized things are only gonna get more visual — and more attention-span challenged — and people typing more than a sentence or two on their phone is going the way of the Dinosaur.

Instagram FAQ #2: Can I Use Instagram on My Laptop?

Uh…sorta. (But they don't make it easy.)

To get started though, you MUST download the Android or iPhone app to your mobile device to be deigned worthy…I mean, be able to register for an Instagram account.

This is done to cut down on the amount of spammy accounts. Or maybe it's just a way to keep businesses away from their prized users. (At least those who won't pay the Instagram advertising toll.)

What you CAN do on your desktop computer is update your information in your all-important bio. (We'll go over this in some detail in the first chapter.)

But for interacting and actually using your Instagram profile, I recommend you do most on your mobile weapon of choice. (If just to ensure what you're putting out there doesn't look like total crap.)

Instagram FAQ #3: Any Weird Instagram Terms I Need to Know About?

Thankfully, Instagram is generally free of the social-media jargon that plagues most social platforms. But here are essential Instagram terms you gotta know:

- **Post** - This is the finished Instagram product after you upload your photo, tweak its appearance and add your caption. This is the jet fuel that makes Instagram go.

- **Filter** - This is the photo filter — what the "kids" call the "old-timey look" — that made Instagram so popular, so fast. (We'll go over filters more later, just know this is the "secret sauce" to Instagram's initial success.)

- **Hashtag** - Like it sounds, this is the word that follows a pound sign (#) which organizes and categorizes Instagram posts. (We'll go over these in more detail later.) They are very important — even more important than hashtags in Twitter.

- **Feed** - The generic term for that unending stream of Instagram goodness produced by the accounts -- and hashtags -- that you follow. (This used to display chronologically -- whatever is newest gets displayed first -- but Instagram is tweaking with alternatives.)

Instagram FAQ #4: Sounds Great...How Do I Make Money With Instagram?

Woah there, Turbo! I love your enthusiasm but ya gotta learn to walk before you run over to the cash register and count your money.

Don't worry: we're gonna go over the nitty-gritty of building your Instagram following and creating killer Instagram content that inspires folks to give you hard currency.

But to satisfy your terminally impatient mind, making money with Instagram is not unlike other social networks, such as Facebook, Twitter or Pinterest:

- Share a bunch of cool photos (Yours included)
- Build up a rabid fan base
- Occasionally share a photo that links to some special offer
- Let your rabid fan base buy your crap
- Rinse and repeat

Instagram FAQ #5: Can Instagram Really Help MY Business?

Unless you're selling "New Coke" or "Blockbuster Video" franchises…yes, it can help.

That said, there's no question Instagram (like Pinterest) caters to products or services that are more aspirational in nature.

Less "I need a personal injury lawyer, so I think I'll go find one on Instagram" and more "Oooh, check out those cool steampunk artisanal socks. Think I'll buy one."

But I've got clients in non-aspirational fields such as mortuary services and life insurance who've used Instagram successfully.

Because what Instagram does really well — besides tell us which rappers are fighting over a girl — is give REAL personality to a business.

And considering Instagram is so damn EASY to use — for both users and devious marketers like ourselves — with just 2-3 minutes a day you can find a new, untapped audience that's just waiting to buy your stuff.

Especially considering how few of your competitors are already on Instagram.

And figuring out how to connect with that untapped audience is what we'll cover in the first chapter.

Introduction Key Takeaways:

- **Instagram is a photo-sharing social network.** Kind of like a souped-up, photo-heavy version of Twitter. (Difference being Instagram actually makes money.)

- **Instagram is popular because it's easy to use, it's got cool photo filters, and it's become the "new" status update.** For many, under 40, it has become the default camera (and social media) app on their phone or tablet.

- **It's all about the mobile experience.** Sure, you can update your bio on your desktop computer, but most of your Instagram duties — including the creation of your account — will be done on your mobile device.

- **There's not much jargon you gotta learn.** (Thank God.) Just the "post," the "filters," the "hashtags" and the "feed."

- **You make money with Instagram by inspiring (or entertaining) people.** And then either let people find your products or services through your bio or subtly throw in a special offer here and there to an excited fan base. (Or both.)

- **Instagram is great at giving a personality to your business.** (Even a faceless, corporate drone army.) And with just a few minutes a day you could see some awesome results.

Chapter 1:
The Art of the Perfect
Instagram Marketing Funnel

"Perfection is not attainable, but if we chase perfection we can catch excellence."

-Vince Lombardi

I know you're just itching to get your Instagram account set up — and browse for that photo filter that will make you look even more amazing and attractive than you are.

But before we do that, we've got a few things to set up. (Namely create ways to turn what we do on Instagram into actual money.)

Having all this in place, before you post your Jack Russell Terrier pics and selfies from your shop, will ensure you don't miss out on possible leads being added to your funnel.

And will help you make progress, even when you don't feel you're making any.

So, here are my 5 Keys to a Kick-Ass Instagram Marketing Funnel:

Instagram Marketing Funnel Key #1: Create a Freebie Thing-a-Majiggy to Give Away

Here's the bitter truth: overt selling on Instagram doesn't work. (I've tried.)

The Instagram crowd is too cynical (and marketing-savvy) to be coerced into heading to your sales page and buy whatever crap you're hawking just because you ask them to.

However, if you give them something for FREE, and it's something they want, you'll not

only find your opt-in conversion rates skyrocket — but you'll make a lot more money (both in the short- and long-term.)

Now what you give away will depend on your business. But here are a couple of things that have worked really well for me:

- Coupon (or discounts)
- Video series
- Special Report
- Cheat Sheet
- Insider Guide
- Resource List

The general rule is, if I'm selling actual merch I'll go with a coupon or discount (either on a specific product or on the entire inventory). If I'm selling education/information, then I'll go with some kind of short, quick-hit insider guide.

Instagram Marketing Funnel Key #2: Have a Way to Collect Email Addresses

You didn't think you were gonna just give that stuff away for FREE for no reason. No, you'll be exchanging that coupon or cheat sheet guide for the most valuable thing a consumer can give you...their email. (Far more valuable than a "Facebook like" or "Instagram follow" any day.)

Now, there are a ton of companies who handle the collection and maintenance of your email marketing efforts. (I use ConvertKit but other ones include iContact and MailChimp.)

Just make sure you've got something, or you'll be leaving money on the Instagram table.

Instagram Marketing Funnel Key #3: Create a Web Page That Collects Email Addresses (in a Non-Sucky Way)

Ya gotta have somewhere to send those people

to get their email address, don't ya? And that's where a dedicated email capture page comes in. (Called a "landing page" in the weird, over-hyped Internet marketing business.)

And this is an AREA where most marketers screw up because they send their prospects to a page on their blog that has way too much CRAP on it.

It'll have their website navigation, sidebars, blog excerpts, social media icons, pictures from their 11th-grade yearbook, etc.

This is the BIGGEST mistake you can make when collecting email subscribers. (And one that'll absolutely SINK your opt-in rates.)

Your email capture page should only have:

- A picture
- A headline (letting people know who the freebie is for)
- A paragraph (telling people what the freebie entails)
- A place for people to type in their name and email

And that's it!

I use a tool called LeadPages —
PunkRockMarketing.com/Lead — which provides
me out-of-the-box templates that make my pages
look awesome. (Without me having to know any
code or contain a scintilla of graphic design talent.)

But you could also use a tool like Instapage. (I've
heard great things about them, and they tend to be
cheaper than LeadPages.)

The nice part about these is they're all mobile-
responsive, so they'll look great across any device.

What I wouldn't do is try to design the page
yourself — or outsource it to somebody else. (The
things you and I don't know about web design would
fill a library. So let's not work on an area that
somebody else has already mastered.)

Instagram Marketing Funnel Key #4: Have Something to Sell on Your Email Subscriber Thank You Page

Here's another BIG mistake marketers make. They go to the trouble of signing somebody up to their email list and then neglect to offer them something to BUY right on the "Thank You" page.

Your "Thank You" page is your most valuable piece of web real estate. After a lead signs up for your list they are at their MOST motivated to buy something from you.

So, why not let them?

Now, I wouldn't offer them your big-ticket $12,000 suite of consulting services. Make it small. (Something under $20.)

But if you set things up right, roughly 25% of the folks who subscribe to your list will buy your first offer. (Which can let you spend more money on advertising than your competition...yeah!)

Note: Both tools I mentioned earlier, LeadPages

and Instapage, let you create snazzy "Thank You" pages that look awesome, and totally convert.

Instagram Marketing Funnel #5: Install Retargeting Code On Your Website

Now, if what I said — "retargeting code" — sounds like something from a bad sci-fi novel, that's okay. Don't worry about the "tech" side. (You can always have somebody far more left-brained and fearful of sunlight than you to handle it.)

This is how "retargeting" works:

- **You place an invisible piece of retargeting code on your ENTIRE website** (This includes your email capture page and your thank you page) — This is easier than it sounds, usually done with a plugin
- **You create a "retargeting" ad —** can be video or text — that reminds people how

awesome your freebie is (and how they'd be
an idiot not to sign up RIGHT NOW)

- **You create "retargeting" ad campaigns**,
  on Google and Facebook, that target folks
  who "visited" one of your pages but did
  NOT reach your "Thank You" page
- **You swim around in your newfound cash**
  (like Scrooge McDuck)

Now, again it's off-topic to go into too much
detail about "retargeting" in this book on Instagram.
But let me tell you, if you haven't tried it, it is
AWESOME.

And at little cost, it will help turn casual window-
shoppers into possible long-term customers.

Chapter One Key Takeaways:

- **Create a freebie that doesn't suck.** (Coupons and discounts work great for physical products. Cheat sheets and insider guides work great for info products.)

- **Have a way to collect email addresses.** If you don't already have an auto-responder, such as ConvertKit or MailChimp, invest in one. It'll be worth it.

- **Build an email lead-capture page that doesn't suck.** All ya want is a headline, brief paragraph describing the freebie, a picture of your freebie, and a box for visitors to sign up for your list. LeadPages and Instapage are great web page template tools for creating these.

- **Offer something to sell on your "Thank You for signing up" page.** (Just don't make it a big-ticket item, something under $20 would work.) This is when people are most motivated to buy something from ya...so don't stand in the way.

- **Install Facebook and Google "retargeting" code on your entire website** — and that includes opt-in and thank you pages. If you don't know how to do this, just hire somebody to do it. (Setting up "retargeting" campaigns based on Instagram visitors is like "found" money.

Chapter 2: Six Steps to a Profitable Instagram Profile

"There's nothing worse than a sharp image of a fuzzy object."

-Ansel Adams

Okay, now you've got a rough understanding of Instagram, let's jump right in with creating you a supremely awesome Instagram profile that not only boosts your exposure — but also lets you collect leads (while you sleep.)

Now, as I mentioned in the last chapter, Instagram is primarily a mobile platform. And much of the Instagram profile creation I'm about to go over will be done on your mobile device of choice.

But the LAST step, the most important step, we're gonna do on your good, old Dinosaur-ish computer. (Remember those?)

So, let's jump right in with my 6 Steps to a Profitable Instagram Profile:

Instagram Profile That Doesn't Suck Step #1: Download the App

I know you need another app on your phone or tablet like you need another hole in the head. (Or another Kardashian spin-off.) But this is the price of doing Instagram business.

And it's easy, just head to your app store and grab the FREE Instagram app. When you open the app, you'll be asked whether you want to SIGN in with Facebook or your email address.

If you plan to have only ONE primary Instagram account, if you've only got one business you're running, then go with the Facebook option. If you're Mark Cuban, helping run 12 different businesses, then go with your email address.

But the choice is entirely yours. Because once you do that, you'll be ready for…

Instagram Profile That Doesn't Suck Step #2: Choose a Non-Sucky Profile Photo

Now, this isn't something you have to do right at this moment. (And you can always go back and change it.) But your profile photo is probably the MOST important factor in your ability to get noticed on Instagram. (That and your ability to get Bruno Mars to mention you in a post.)

Here's what you gotta know about Instagram profile photos:

- **The ideal size for a profile photo is 500x500 pixels.** Anything smaller and you'll look more pixelated than a Minecraft game.
- **Your profile photo will be resized to a square ratio.** So, if you don't want to look

like you've been decapitated, size your bio photo to 500x500 before uploading.

- **If the account is gonna represent a corporate brand, go for a simple logo (without words.)** Forget that picture of your team on the front steps, or that logo with the text at 4-point font. (It'll look crappy on a phone.) Just stick with a simple, eye-catching logo.

- **If the account is gonna represent YOU as a brand, go for a high-quality photo that shows you off.** Avoid head-to-toe shots, unless you're a fitness instructor and you wanna show off your six-pack abs. Otherwise go for a shoulder-up shot that shows off that winning smile of yours. (Or in my case, slightly exasperated grin.)

- **Go easy with filters on your bio photo.** We're gonna go over filters in more detail later but try to avoid going heavy with the filters on your bio photo. (They can make your pic look too dark.)

You can also grab a photo from Facebook or snap a quick selfie right there in the app. Just ask yourself: "would I buy something from somebody who spent less than 10 seconds on their Instagram profile pic?"

Instagram Profile That Doesn't Suck Step #3: Find Some Friends (If You Have Some)

Right after you create your profile you'll be taken to a screen called "Find Friends." (If only that screen were available when I was in high school.)

You DON'T have to choose this option at the moment you create your profile. You can always go back later and select the "Find Friends" feature from your profile.

But there are three powerful options Instagram offers here to find friends:

1. Find friends from your Facebook account (Did we mention Facebook owns Instagram?)
2. Find friends from your phone contact list
3. Find friends from your email address

Unless you're Edward Snowden — or you want none of your inner circle knowing what you do for a living — I recommend you take advantage of this powerful tool.

It'll make getting some serious traction with your posts much easier down the road.

Instagram Profile That Doesn't Suck Step #4: Choose a Username That Doesn't Suck

So, before I give you my tips on creating a username, let me be clear right at the start.

In the Instagram world, "username" and "personal name" are different. (Confused? Yeah, I was too, the first time.)

The username is your Instagram handle —
Example: "@facebookceo" — while the personal
name is just what it sounds like, your name —
Example: "Mark Zuckerberg."

The personal name field is simple, use your
name. (Or whatever alias you're using to evade the
cops.) And you can change this information as many
times as you want.

But it's your username that will drive much of
the "branding juice" of your Instagram account. And
it can be rather challenging to find the right
username, especially if somebody has already taken
one related to your given name or your business.
(Welcome to the "Wild West" of social media.)

If you're having a tough time finding that perfect
username then here are a couple of pointers:

- **Use periods (".") and underscores ("_")
  between words to help you find a unique
  username.** This won't always work — with
  my name "Michael Clarke" I only happen to
  be competing with 4 million other people —

but it can be beneficial in the right situation.

- **Add a "The" or "The Real" prefix to your name or business.** This is a trick I got from a LinkedIn seminar. (The seminar was horrible except for that one tip.) If Joe Schmidt is taken, maybe it's time you embrace your inner superhero and become "TheJoeSchmidt" or "TheRealJoeSchmidt."
- **If your company name is taken add a ".com" to the end of it.** Or ".org" or whatever the extension of your domain is. Not only can it let you hold on to your branding identity, but it also (not-so-subtly) encourages folks to check out your website.

Instagram Profile That Doesn't Suck Step #5: Create That All-Important Bio

Of the five steps in this chapter, creating your bio is by far the most important. That's because your bio is not only where you get to throw in some keywords related to your business or field, but it's also where you get to place that all-important call-to-action. (And where you get to add a juicy link back to your website.)

Now, as I alluded to before, it is POSSIBLE to update your bio through your mobile device, but I don't recommend it. That's because adding text to your bio, through your mobile device, will CLUMP all the text together.

No matter how many times you hit the return key, Instagram doesn't seem to recognize line breaks when it comes to your bio.

So, what's an enterprising marketer to do? Simply update your bio — on your desktop computer — using this simple process:

1. **Download a FREE copy of my Instagram bio text template.** You can find it at PunkRockMarketing.com/InstagramBio. This is a simple text document to ensure your line breaks and formatting is just how

you want it.

2. **Use the template to fill in the relevant info for your bio.** I recommend line #1 of your bio be used to describe your role in the business ("Author. Entrepreneur. International Man of Mystery") and lines #2-#4 be used to craft a CTA (call-to-action) that gets people to act ("To grab a FREE copy of my special report: "7 Ways to Download a Special Report") head over to:")

3. **Head over to https://instagram.com/accounts/edit/#** and log in to Instagram.

4. **Paste in text from your Instagram bio template EXACTLY,** adding no additional characters or line breaks.

5. **In the website field, insert the relevant web page** you're asking people to visit (This will automatically show up as the final line in your bio.)

6.   Click "Save" and you're good to go.

Now that's the HOW of setting up your Instagram bio. But that doesn't tell us the WHAT, what the heck should we be pitching in our Instagram bio. (What's the best way for us to use that space in an effective and profitable way?)

Well, this will depend on your particular business model. But here are a couple thoughts to keep in mind:

- **Resist the urge to hawk multiple things in the same bio.** If you want people to "like" you on Facebook, do that. If you want people to try your "Columbia House 12 CDs for a penny" offer, do that. Don't do both. (The confused mind always says no.)

- **Links to sales page and offers — unless it's an irresistible offer — tend to NOT work.** Now this might not be a deal-breaker for you. Perhaps your sales page offer is so inviting, and your conversion rates so high, that all ya need is eyeballs. But mostly anything over $10, direct sales links don't convert that awesomely.

- **Free giveaways or super-cheap offers work REALLY well.** If you've got ANY way to spin your product or service into something free(ish) then go for that in your Instagram bio. (Will pay off huge down the line.)

- **If you have nothing to give away**, you could always just ask people to "follow your account" or "like your pictures" or follow you on any number of other social media channels. (Snapchat and Pinterest work really well — others not so much.)

- **Don't just encourage people to "Check out your website" or "subscribe to your newsletter."** Nobody cares about you. They want to know what's in it for them. So give them a reason to check out your stuff, beyond the fact you finally figured out how to FTP a WordPress website.

- **Use active verbs to tell people what you want them to do.** Don't be shy. (Nobody on Instagram is.) Tell people exactly, what you want them to do. "Download your FREE report; Click to grab your complimentary offer; Buy every single product I sell...Now!"

Instagram Profile That Doesn't Suck Step #6: Link Up Your Instagram Account With Your Other Social Media Channels

You don't have to do this now; you can do it later. But at some point, you'll want to sync up your Instagram account with your social media accounts — including Facebook, Twitter, Tumblr and Flickr.

This will make the sharing of your posts to your various social media properties way easier. (And you'll boost your engagement and reach of your posts without having to do a damn thing.)

Just REMEMBER not to go all "Andrew Dice Clay" with your Instagram posts. (Your grandmother might see it on Facebook and you won't get that $5 check for Christmas.)

Chapter Two Key Takeaways:

- **Ya gotta create your Instagram account on a mobile device.** Price of doing business, don't stress it.

- **To create a profile photo that doesn't suck remember to resize your image to 500x500 pixels.** (Otherwise it'll look Pixelated.) Also, keep it simple with non-text logos and head shots.

- **Use the "Find Friends" feature to locate people** in your email contact list or Facebook friend list who you can add to your Instagram tribe.

- **Creating a username that doesn't suck is harder than it sounds.** (Many names are already taken.) IF you're stumped, use periods/underscores, domain extensions or a simple "The" or "TheReal" prefix to get around this.

- **For your bio make sure to a) update it on**

your computer (not mobile device) b) Use my FREE Instagram Bio text document to keep formatting correct (PunkRockMarketing.com/InstagramBio) c) Just pitch ONE THING in your bio.

- **Sync your Instagram account with your other social media accounts**, such as your Twitter, Facebook, Tumblr and Flickr accounts.

Chapter 3:

Spying on the Competition for Fun and Profit

"A horse never runs so fast as when it has other horses to outpace it."

-Ovid

Okay, so we've got your Instagram profile set up and your bio looking spiffy and chock-full of marketing potential.

But before you shoot pics and uploading your Instagram posts of awesomeness, there's ONE important task to complete. And that is to…

…blatantly SPY on your competition! (But in an

ethical way.)

Not only will it give you ideas on the kinds of Instagram content you SHOULD — and should NOT — create, but it will also give you some much-needed intel on the best way to get your content discovered. (Which #hashtags should accompany your content.)

So, here are my 3 keys to spying…err…researching what your industry is currently doing on Instagram:

(Note: I know you're tempted to skip this part. But resist that inner teenager inside ya who wants to just go play video games. This will make you money down the road.)

Instagram Spying Key #1: Learn the Ways of the Enemy

One of the quickest ways to learn the Instagram mores of your target audience is to figure out how competitors are ALREADY communicating with your target audience on Instagram.

This includes paying attention to things like:

- How often do they post on Instagram? (Every day? Twice a week? Once every Presidential election?)
- What kind of CTA (call-to-action) do they have in their Instagram bio? (If any)
- What kinds of #hashtags do they include with their posts? (Are their #hashtags unique to their brand? Or are they "popular" #hashtags intended to throw a much-wider Instagram net?)
- What kinds of Instagram content do they share? (Product shots, behind-the-scenes stuff, blatant offers and coupons, how-to content, stuff created by their fans, etc.)
- And what things would you like to STEAL from their campaigns? (And what would you never, under any circumstances STEAL?)

Now to make this process easier, I've created an

Instagram Marketing Research excel sheet, which you can grab TOTALLY FREE by heading over to PunkRockMarketing.com/InstagramResearch.

All you gotta do is:

- Head over to Instagram
- Type in keywords related to your business (or if you already know a competitor is on Instagram, put them in)
- Find at least 5 competitors (who have a minimum of 1000 followers)
- Scan their bios and photo feed (and fill out your Instagram Research sheet)

Now you DON'T want to copy every single thing these brands do. (Many have no frickin' clue what they're doing with Instagram.)

In the Instagram Marketing Research sheet I give you some examples I did with those high fructose syrup giants - Coke, Pepsi, and Dr. Pepper.

Even with these huge multi-billion-dollar companies I still don't love everything they do. (I love Coke's use of user-generated content and their clear CTA in their bio. But their photos feel too "artsy" and "couture" for me.)

And Pepsi may evoke a nice family-friendly, holiday BBQ feel that ties in with their demographic. But that their bio has no CTA is mind-boggling.)

But doing this exercise — should only take you 20 minutes — will give you a virtual B.A. in Instagram Studies. (Without the need to take out a single student loan.)

Instagram Spying Key #2: Find Your Future Partners

So, once ya got your list of competitors, it's time to up your game and get your full-on Master's Degree in Instagram Studies. And you do that by making a mongo list of Instagram influencers.

Now, these are not competitors. These are brands and/or personalities who are related to your business.

For instance if I was a golf club manufacturer, then influencers would include:

- Golf pros
- Golf instructors
- Golf courses
- Golf magazines
- Golf bloggers

...folks who have an audience that is interested in what I offer. (But are not in direct competition.)

And don't forget about "Instagram enthusiasts" who simply LOVE (or pretend to love) everything about a topic related to your business.

These folks can have HUGE follower counts — some over a million — and will even "sell" a sponsored shout-out to their audience.

For now just dig through Instagram by:

- Type a keyword related to your business in the Instagram search bar
- Find 5-10 influencers with at least 1000 followers (Keep searching until you find a

decent mix of magazines, websites, bloggers, enthusiasts, manufacturers, etc.)

- Scan their profiles, and input their info in your Instagram Research sheet, under the "Influencers" tab (Grab their email or social contact info, if provided)

Instagram Spying Key #3: Make a List of All-Powerful Hashtags

Once you've done some early reconnaissance on the competition and influencers who might help you down the line...

...it's time to make your master list of hashtags you'll be using for each of your Instagram posts.

Huh? Hashtags? Do I really have to do this?

Uh...yeah.

See, in the Instagram universe #hashtags are valuable currency. (Even more valuable than they are on other social platforms such as Pinterest or Twitter.)

Because there is just NO more reliable way to get your Instagram posts discovered than to have a ton of #hashtags.

And here's the interesting part about Instagram #hashtags:

- Studies show the MORE hashtags you have, the MORE your posts get engaged with

- Instagram allows you up to 30 hashtags per post. (I recommend keeping the number around 15-20, but still that's a lot of hashtag real estate we can be using.)

- Hashtags are best — just like your stock portfolio — when they're diverse. (Meaning you should have a mix of mega-popular hashtags, semi-popular hashtags, and less-popular hashtags.

The good news is hardly anybody goes to this much trouble when including hashtags in their posts. (Which lets you and I take advantage of their ignorance and get our posts to the front of the

Instagram line.)

So, here's what ya do:

- Open up that Instagram Research Worksheet (head over to the third tab, entitled "Hashtags")
- Head to Instagram and type keywords in the search bar related to your business.
- Your goal is to find FIVE hashtags with at least 1000 results, FIVE hashtags with under 1000 results, and FIVE hashtags with under 100 results (This doesn't have to be exact but get as close as you can.)
- Include your own branded hashtags in the sheet — this will probably be related to your company name or hashtag slogans you've used in the past

Now this Master List of Kick-Ass Hashtags will evolve as you get more familiar with Instagram. (You may find new ones or take some off the list.)

But try your best to get a nice, diverse mix of

hashtags that can leverage super-popular hashtags and slightly less-popular hashtags.

If you're able to complete your Instagram Research worksheet, and I know you are, then you will be ahead of 92.6% of all the other marketers out there. You'll have a Ph.D. in Instagram Marketing Readiness.

And then the next step will be creating some killer Instagram content, which is what we'll cover in the next chapter.

Chapter Three Key Takeaways:

- **The best way to learn the ins and outs of Instagram is to study the competition.** (Warts and all.) Find out when and how often they post, along with ideas on content (and what they promote.)

- **Another key resource are influencers, profiles that have an audience who'd be interested in your products, but not in direct competition with you.** These can be things like blogs, magazines, websites, manufacturers and deranged enthusiasts.

- **Hashtags are super-important in Instagram.** So collect a batch of hashtags you can use for your future posts. (Try your best to find a mix of popular, semi-popular, and somewhat niche hashtags to help your discoverability.)

Chapter 4:

Seven Ways to Create Killer Instagram Content

"Creativity is knowing how to hide your sources."
-C.E.M. Joad

Okay, we're here! We're finally gonna create some visually delicious, lead-generatin' Instagram content!

But before I share with you my 7 Secrets to Creating Killer Instagram Content — and I use these secrets over and over — I need to lay out my...

[BORING BUT IMPORTANT LEGAL DISCLAIMER]

I know the Internet can feel like the "Wild West" sometimes. But Instagram has made it a priority to crack down on people posting photos they don't hold the rights to.

And though Instagram tends to be a bit conservative, as social media companies go, it's their sandbox. (So we need to play by their rules.)

That means:

- Don't grab a photo off the Internet and post it to Instagram, without the permission of the rights holder. (Usually they'll give it to you, if you ask.)

- If you get permission to use the photo, be sure to credit them in the caption.

- Don't assume adding a "filter" to an existing photo makes it "yours." It doesn't.

- When in doubt, grab a photo from one of the many royalty-free photo collections out there. (Such as MorgueFile, Wikipedia, or Pixabay.)

- The EASIEST way around this conundrum

is to simply take your own photos.

Got it? Don't post photos unless ya got permission.

And if you want to use a photo that you didn't take, grab it from one of the royalty-free sites.

Okay, enough of the boring legal stuff. Let's jump right in with...

Killer Instagram Content Method #1: Show Off Your Products & Services (in Context)

This is probably the MOST effective Instagram marketing strategy there is, showing off your product or service in all its glory. But most companies who do this, execute it so clumsily they hardly get any marketing bang from it. (Which is a shame.)

Here's how to strut your company stuff (effectively):

- **Go for pictures of humans**

using/interacting with your products NOT staged product shots. Try to put a person in the shot when featuring your products. It boosts engagement and leads to higher conversions.

- **Your team IS a part of your products and services.** So, why not show off that hard-working (or moderately hard-working) staff of yours? Studies have shown that the more people know about a company's employees, the more likely they are to buy...so why not use it to your advantage?

- **Before-and-after shots work great.** If your business revolves around some kind of transformation — whether physical fitness or interior decorating — add great "before-and-after" photos to underscore the power of your product or service. (In Chapter 7, I'll go over tools that can help you create these types of pictures.)

- **Photos from live events and product**

launches work really well. You and I both know how boring business events can be, but our audience doesn't have to know that. Have somebody take a bunch of pics of your event and throw them up on Instagram. (This boosts your presence as an authority and gives you Instagram content you can use for weeks.)

- **Humor goes a long way with your product/service photos.** There is so much blatant self-promotion on Instagram, it's refreshing to see a business who brings wit and self-deprecation to their product pics. So, don't take yourself, or your business, too seriously. And have fun (while you promote.)

Killer Instagram Content Method #2: Promote Your Events or Limited-Time Offers

This is what MOST companies love to share on Instagram: endless posts about whatever promo crap they're hawking. And these types of posts CAN be profitable (if you do them right.)

Here's what I've learned about doing a few hundred of these:

- **Don't assume people will get the message of your offer from your caption.** You GOTTA put a text overlay on the image that spells out exactly what the offer is.

- **Don't put TOO MUCH text over the image.** Keep it simple. Use active verbs that indicate clear benefits. And let your sales page do the talking.

- **Include time-limits or discounted prices in your image.** Make it urgent that people CLICK NOW, not later, to check out your stuff. (Scarcity and discounts work really well.)

- **Pictures of people enjoying your event or**

product work best for overall promotion.
Far better than boring, generic product
photos.

- **Short videos are a great way to boost
  interest in your event or product launch.**
  Hardly anybody does these. Which is fine
  with me — lets you and kick serious
  marketing ass. The key with these is to sell
  your "excitement" — not the product. (Let
  your sales page do the heavy lifting.)

- **Tease events and product launches in
  the days leading up with some
  Instagram posts.** I have no idea why
  people would be interested in watching us
  "prepare" for a launch or event — but they
  do. (Trust me.) So build anticipation with
  pre-launch videos and images that let people
  know WHEN it's coming.

- **Tell people EXACTLY what they need
  to do to get your offer.** "Click here to…"
  or "To grab your FREE offer…" Don't be

vague. Tell people what you WANT them to do. (And they'll usually do it.)

Killer Instagram Content Method #3: Inspirational (Feel-Good) Crap

These types of posts are created by putting inspirational quotes in a text overlay over a photo of a sunrise. Or a mountain. Or a redwood forest. (Man, they love redwood forests.)

And I, personally, find these vapid and annoying. But I am in the vast, cynical minority.

But here are a few tips to keep in mind:

- **To create these quote posts use a tool, such as Canva or PicMonkey.** These are FREE tools that let you easily cobble together a textured background image (with your devastating quote of choice.)

- **If you can, pick a quote from a speaker most of your audience has heard of.** That insight from that 19th-century physicist may be profound, but its impact will be lessened if nobody has heard of 'em.

- **Pick a short, clever quote.** Don't go with a super-long paragraph on a topic. Keep it short and simple.

- **Find quotes at sites like Brainy Quotes or GoodReads.** These are good, FREE places to find quotes to use with your feel-good crap.

- **Pick a quote that has resonance with your audience.** If you're selling fitness equipment, go with something about "goal-setting" or "determination." If you're selling financial services, go with something about "wisdom" and "experience." Choose the right bait for the right fish.

- **When in doubt, go with something about "overcoming adversity."** That's something we can all relate to. (No matter what kind of crap we're looking to buy.)

Killer Instagram Content Method #4: Random, Personal Stuff About Your Day-to-Day

This is another category I could do without. (But I'm a cranky malcontent who spends time in his bunker waiting for the zombie apocalypse.)

People love getting to know more about people. And that includes:

- What movies you're watching
- Books you're reading
- Struggles you've overcome
- Goals you've accomplished
- Anything to do with kids and/or pets (This stuff is Instagram crack)
- Those ever-annoying "selfies" of wherever you are throughout the day

I know. Sounds like 5th ring of hell stuff. But people love commenting and liking this crap.

And, when you think about it, one of the most

powerful motivators in the world is the "need" to be valuable. To contribute something to the tribe. (And for a lot of folks, this makes them feel like they're contributing something, even if they're just sitting on their be-hind.)

Killer Instagram Content Method #5: Sharing Your How-to Expertise

Your business may not use content marketing much. (You know that annoying method where you give away your best stuff — so they're tempted to buy some of your crappier stuff for money.)

But there's nothing people LOVE more than learning secrets, tips, strategies, and shortcuts that'll help them feel smarter than other people...I mean...lead better and more impactful lives.

Couple things to keep in mind when promoting content with an Instagram post:

- **Videos and photo galleries do well** when promoted on Instagram. 5200-word essays?

Not so much.

- **Pair a benefit-focused text overlay with an eye-catching image** to promote your content. And by "benefit," we mean a "benefit" to the user…not you. (Just sayin'.)
- **Use a benefit-focused headline that doesn't sound like homework.** I know the headline of your blog post may be "124 Ways to Improve Your Life." But keep it simple. Use phrases like "Discover the #1 Secret…"; "Learn my #1 Strategy…" Keep it simple and non-threatening.
- **Try to have the image you use in your Instagram post be the SAME** as the one featured on the webpage you're promoting. This is an overlooked technique, but you wanna make the transition from Instagram to website as quickly as possible. (And using the same creative will help that.)
- **Make it clear what KIND of content you're promoting (especially if you're**

promoting a PHOTO or VIDEO.) For some, and by some I mean most, people just don't want to click on something that sounds like work. But photos and video don't sound like work, they sound like goofing off.

Killer Instagram Content Method #6: Ask for User-Generated Content

This might be the MOST under-utilized type of Instagram content there is. Which is a shame because it's not only content you DON'T have to create — but it also boosts the engagement of your audience.

And user-generated content like this can come in many forms:

- Users submitting photos of them using your product
- Users submitting photos of them striking a unique or interesting pose (This works really well — no idea why)

- Users giving feedback on a question you pose
- Users creating a video response to one of your posts
- Users/customers giving video testimonials

And that LAST ONE is worth its weight in gold. (And worth more than 100 sales pages combined.)

Now, this strategy won't be effective until you've amassed somewhat of a following on Instagram. (And in Chapter 6, we'll go over methods for building your Instagram zombie army.)

But all you gotta do is just upload an eye-catching photo — with a text overlay "asking' people to upload their own photo and adding a branded hashtag of your choosing — and you've got your every own content marketing army. (Without having to break a sweat.)

Killer Instagram Content Method #7: Good, Old Video

So, we've touched on video in the first six Instagram content methods. But I want to encourage you to give video a try. (And the Instagram app makes it so damn easy. Just hit the record button and then the pause button and you've shot a scene.)

Now the maximum time allowed for Instagram videos is 60 seconds. (So, no Presidential convention speeches allowed.) But I've seen clever things done with videos on Instagram:

- Answer a single question
- Offer a single tip
- Show off a singular fitness trick (or dance move)
- Give a daily update on what's going on in somebody's lives
- Give customers a chance to express their opinion, show off their creativity or offer a testimonial

If you're a cantankerous English major like me
— who reads 1200-page 19th-century novels for fun!
— then this 60-second limit to videos will seem like
a sign of the impending fall of civilization.

But to many of your would-be customers, it is
the perfect length for them to get a taste of what you
(or your business) is all about. And the companies
that are able to manage this short (but powerful)
method of communication are poised to make a crap
load of money. (Pretty good for 60 seconds of your
time.)

Chapter Four Key Takeaways:

- **One of the best ways to use Instagram is to show your products or services in context.** (And by "in context" we mean actual, breathing humans using your stuff, not just stock-photo models.)

- **Promoting live-events and special offers is another great way to use Instagram.** Just be sure the KEY information is in a text overlay on the image. (Don't expect the caption to do all the work.)

- **Inspirational (touchy-feely) quote posts work well on Instagram.** (Even though I hate 'em.) Just use a tool like Canva or PicMonkey, and throw a short, clever quote from a speaker "some" people have heard of.

- **Random, personal (but not-too-personal) snapshots of your day are another great way to engage with your audience.** (Doesn't necessarily have an immediate ROI, but can build some serious goodwill later on down the line.)

- **Promoting your how-to content — especially videos — on Instagram can seriously boost your marketing.** Just be sure to indicate the benefit of the content (and whether it's a video) in the text overlay on the image.

- **User-generated content can be some of the most powerful and easiest type of content to create.** Just ask your followers to respond to questions, show off their style, film themselves using your products...just be sure to wait until you got a decent following first.

- **Posting videos straight to Instagram is an under-utilized — yet staggeringly effective — form of marketing.** Yeah, you only get 60 seconds, but it works really well for testimonials, behind-the-scenes tidbits, and quick mini-tips.

Chapter 5:

The Perfect Instagram Post Checklist

"It takes real planning to organize this kind of chaos."
-Mel Odom

All the prep work is done. We're (finally) going to upload your delicious Instagram content for the world to see! (And hopefully inspire them to buy some of our crap.)

In the next chapter we'll delve into the creation of your Instagram fan base and go over how to attract those smartphone-addicted masses to follow — and engage — with your Instagram activity.

But BEFORE THAT I encourage you to upload at least 10-15 posts FIRST. And for Instagram posting, feel free to follow my Perfect Instagram Post Checklist.

This is the 7-step checklist I use each time I post my Instagram goodness, and it'll ensure you maximize the potential of your posts — and wring every ounce of marketing juice out of your Instagram marketing efforts.

So, without further Instagram adieu, let's jump right in with:

Instagram Post Checklist Item #1: Pick a Goal That Doesn't Suck

Now, you need not spend hours on this. (Please don't.) But it's a good idea to have SOME idea what the hell you're trying to accomplish with a particular marketing activity, before actually doing it.

And with Instagram posts the goals will usually be from the following list:

- Boost exposure for a product or service (Product/service shots, behind-the-scenes, videos)
- Increase engagement with your Instagram account (Questions, Feel-good quotes, contests, user-generated content)
- Gather sign-ups for your email list (How-to content, free offers)
- Drive sales (promoted events, product launches, behind-the-scenes videos, user-generated content)
- Ramp up exposure for your other social media properties (videos, behind-the-scenes, feel-good quotes, user-generated content)
- Pad your Instagram follower account (Almost any type of post)

The key thing to remember is that an Instagram post CAN have multiple goals. (You can sell stuff AND pad your Instagram follower count.)

But I like to have ONE primary goal and 1-2 tertiary goals. And, for my business, my THREE most successful goals are:

1. Gather sign-ups for my email list
2. Increase engagement
3. Boost exposure

Direct selling from my Instagram account doesn't always pay off for me. (I prefer to do that through my email marketing.) But your funnel might support linking to a sales page.

And I don't focus too much on increasing my Instagram follower count with a specific post. (That happens anyway.)

But you'll want to tweak and test to see what works for your business. Just get in the habit of choosing ONE primary goal — and 1-2 tertiary goals. (Don't I just sound like an English major with my throwin' around "tertiary?")

Instagram Post Checklist Item #2: Pick a Posting Time That Doesn't Suck

Okay, now we're getting to some juicy ninja-hack stuff. WHEN should we be posting our Instagram stuff?

To be fair, Instagram is such a NEW platform — and the user base will change as it gets adopted by people who are over 30 and don't have lip piercings — but for now the best data suggests that optimal Instagram posting times of the week are (in descending order):

1. Wednesday
2. Thursday
3. Tuesday

With "Mondays" being the absolute WORST day of the week. (I think that's because most Instagram users are hungover…uh…I mean, focusing on their work.)

But if you can only do 1-2x a week — be sure to

post somewhere in that Tuesday-Thursday range.

Now, when it comes to time of day, there are essentially THREE sweet spots:

- 5:00 p.m. (EST)
- 10:00 p.m. (EST)
- 1:00-2:00 a.m. (EST)

This will depend on your particular audience, and their nocturnal habits. But try these out first, and then do your own testing. Again, if you're only gonna post a couple times a week, you could do worse than follow these general industry benchmarks. (And in Chapter 7, I'll show you some super-simple apps you can use to schedule all your Instagram goodness.)

Instagram Post Checklist Item #3: Upload That Photo and Make It All Pretty-Like

The HOW to upload your photo is very simple. (So simple a Kardashian could handle it.) You:

- Open Instagram on your phone or tablet
- Click on the big blue camera button (or click on the "+" button on the bottom)
- Find the photo on your device using "library"
- …and upload

But it's those all-important Instagram filters I want to walk you through. Because they can be confusing, and unless you've got some serious photography skills you'll spend THREE hours trying to find the right filter. (Or you'll end up with Instagram posts that make you look like a zombie.)

So, here are a few things I've learned about Instagram filters (and again I'm no photo-filter expert!)

- **Don't just stick with the "Normal" filter.** It's boring and nobody will love you. (Okay, maybe that's strong. But go crazy…it's Instagram!)
- **When in doubt, go for the "Earlybird"**

filter. It's the most forgiving — makes you look more "bronzed" and "golden" than usual — and it's the most popular filter out there for a reason. It makes every shot look dramatic and interesting.

- **If you want your picture to look dramatic** and have dark edges around the corner — like an old-time photograph --go for "X-Pro II."

- **If you don't want a "dark" photo and you want to boost the "lightness" of your pics** — and I'm thinking mostly here of product launches, event promotions, and links to content — then go with "Valencia." (It's a dramatic filter, without the "undead" look.)

- **Go with "Hefe" if your picture has lots of color and you need sharpness and vibrancy.** And not "bright" in a hipster band photo sort of way.

- **If you're going for that artistic,**

discolored (post-apocalyptic wasteland) look, where the color is washed out, then "Brannan" is your filter of choice.

- **And finally if you wanna go "light" with the filters** and use the Instagram bells-and-whistles, then "Nashville" is a great add to your Instagram toolbox.

But again, don't take hours and hours poring over all the filters. Just try a few out and see if you like the results. (And when you're posting something that requires immediate action, go easy on the hipster, starving-artist filters.)

Note: If you don't see any of the filters I mentioned above, click on "manage" to specify which filters you see in your dashboard.

Instagram Post Checklist Item #4: Create a Killer Caption

Aside from the photo you take, this is the MOST important part of the Instagram posting process. That's because your caption has to do so many things:

- Tell people what the picture is about
- Ask people to comment and/or share your post
- Add a call to action (if relevant)
- Add those all-important hashtags (15-20 if ya got them)

I know this seems daunting. And the first couple of these you do may appear awkward and ineffective. But stick with the process I'm about to show you and you'll master creating captions in no time. (And you can always go back and edit your captions later if you screw up.)

So, here's what I do:

1. **Open your Facebook app on your phone or tablet.** Huh? Facebook? Yeah, we're gonna type our status update there, so it recognizes any line breaks we add. Otherwise our caption will look more

scrunched than a rush-hour NYC subway. I know this seems like a pain — and you don't have to do it if you don't want to — but once you get used to it you'll see it pay dividends.

2. **Start off by telling folks about the back story of the picture.** (Don't start off promoting.) Nobody cares about YOUR marketing. But do they care about your story — the WHY you took the picture? Where you were WHY you took it. And WHAT you were thinking when you took it. ("Here's my view from the hotel lobby of the Waldorf Astoria in NYC at the Evil James Bond Villain Convention!")

3. **Hit "return" and add a line break.**

4. **(Optional) Add your CTA (call-to-action).** This will either be a) Click on this link to get more info or buy something or b) Comment, like and share this post. (Or both.) Either way make it friendly but

CLEAR what you want them to do. ("If you'd like to find out how to be a James Bond villain get my FREE "How to Be a James Bond Villain" report by clicking on the link in my profile."; "What would your James Bond villain name be? Let us know in the comments!"

5. **Hit "return" and add a line break.**

6. **Add them Hashtags.** You should already have a nice list of hashtags assembled. (I recommend having them in a text document in a cloud storage app like Dropbox, so you can easily copy and paste them.)

7. **Copy and paste the text from the Facebook app to your Instagram caption.** And you've completed your first caption!

Note: Instagram does NOT allow you to embed links right in your caption. (No bueno.) But in Chapter 7, I'll show you a super-sneaky ninja way to get links right in the caption.

Instagram Post Checklist Item #5: Tag Other Instagram Users

This won't be entirely relevant when you're first starting out and have no followers to speak of. But tagging other Instagram users, who might be interested in what you're posting, is a cool way to get INSTANT engagement. (And build your follower base in no time.)

Again, not required, but it's nice if you like to engage and talk with other human beings.

Instagram Post Checklist Item #6: Tag Your Geographic Location

You wouldn't think this was important. God knows I don't care WHERE somebody is posting from.

But having a geo-verified Instagram post has proven to boost both engagement and conversion rates. Maybe it's like a subtle form of account verification.

Whatever it is, unless you're in the Witness

Protection program and want nobody to know where you are, tag your geographic location.

Instagram Post Checklist Item #6: Promote Your Post on Your Other Social Media Sites

As we went over in Chapter 2, you can link up your Instagram account with your Twitter, Tumblr, Flickr and Facebook accounts. (There are also a bunch of other accounts I've never heard of.)

Now you DON'T have to share your Instagram posts on these other platforms. (And you can pick which ones you want to use for promotion at the time of posting.)

But unless you go off your meds and are knee-deep in a Charlie Sheen-esque rant…why not? Give your posts as much exposure as you can.

Chapter Five Key Takeaways:

- **You can have more than one goal for your Instagram posts.** But keep it limited to one or two primary goals. My favorite goals are boosting exposure for a product, increasing engagement on my account, and gathering sign-ups.

- **Tuesday-Thursdays (5:00 p.m. and 10:00 p.m. EST) are the best times of the week to post on Instagram.** Avoid Mondays if you can.

- **Add "some" kind of filter to your Instagram posts.** (Normal filters are boring.) There are many to choose from, but if in doubt go for "Earlybird."

- **The ideal Instagram caption tells people what the pictures are about, asks folks to comment, provides a call-to-action and has 15-20 relevant hashtags.** (Don't forget to create your post captions away from your smartphone, if possible.)

- **Tagging other Instagram users with your posts is a great way to boost engagement** and show super-cheap social proof.

- **Don't forget to promote your Instagram posts on your other social media sites.** That includes Twitter, Tumblr, Flickr and Facebook.

Chapter 6:

How to Create a Rabid Tribe of Zombie Instagram Followers

"A friend is someone who knows all about you and still loves you."

-Elbert Hubbard

Congratulations! If you've read this far that means you're in the upper 75% of all breathing humans on the planet. (Most of whom never read more than half of ANY book...EVER!)

Hopefully, you've dipped your toe into the Instagram waters. (And picked up a few followers along the way, by simply being an awesome person.)

But in this chapter we're gonna put that Instagram tribe-buildin' muscle of yours on steroids. (And we're gonna do that with my seven favorite strategies for acquiring an Instagram zombie army…I mean…passionate Instagram following:

Instagram Tribe Buildin' Tip #1: Post More Than You Think You Should

I know this is gonna sound obvious — which it is — but the MORE ya post on Instagram, the more you get noticed. (And add to that zombie army.)

Instagram is more like Twitter and Facebook, than it is Pinterest. Though posts can be found through #hashtag searches, recent content ALWAYS gets noticed and consumed far more than older stuff. (And with the attention span of most Instagram users hovering somewhere near that of a housefly, it's no surprise that consistent content is the key to getting discovered.)

In the last chapter I went over general guidelines about optimal times of the week to post (Tuesdays and Thursday evenings) but once you get the hang of this…

…as long as you're saying something interesting, post as much as you damn well want. (Nobody'll throw you in Instagram jail — and you might just get a ton more sales.)

Instagram Tribe Buildin' Tip #2: Put a "Follow Me On Instagram" Button on Your Website

The actual creation of the button is super simple. Just head over to ShareThis.com, put in your account name, specify your text ("Follow Me/Us on Instagram" works) and it'll spit out a gorgeous piece of code you can put on your website. (Best of all, ShareThis lets you create buttons for all the major social platforms. Nice!)

Though you can certainly put the "Follow Me on Instagram" code wherever you want, I would absolutely recommend you put it in places such as:

- Your website sidebar
- The footer of each of your blog posts
- Any "About Me" Pages on your website

But you shouldn't just stop with your website. You could also put it in…

- Your Tumblr posts
- Your Twitter bio
- Your email signature
- Your message board profiles
- Anywhere else you can think of!

Now, your audience may not be super Instagram-savvy…yet. But don't worry, in a year your efforts as an Instagram marketing pioneer will pay off.

Instagram Tribe Buildin' Tip #3: Like, Follow and Comment Your Way to Stardom

This is probably the MOST EFFECTIVE way to build your fan base. But it's not an overnight strategy, and requires spending short, consistent bursts of time interacting with fellow users on Instagram. (I know, not exactly a "night at the movies.")

But here's how it works:

- Find a batch of Instagram users you want to interact with. Either use a relevant hashtag (such as #socialmedia) or just head to the followers of an influencer your target audience would be likely to follow. (You should have a list of influencers in your Instagram Research Worksheet we went over in Chapter 3.)

- Scanning the list of users, follow SIX

accounts who fall into the demographic and interest patterns of your ideal audience. (Tip: Make sure they've got at least 500 followers themselves, and at least a line or two in their bio. Otherwise they probably spend little time on Instagram.)

- For THREE of the SIX followers you just followed, check out their posts and "like" at least THREE, per user. (To "like" a post just click on the "heart" icon in the lower left.)

- For the OTHER THREE followers you just followed, check out their posts and "comment" on at least ONE of their posts. (Be sure it's not a generic "nice post" comment. But something unique and authentic…and something a robot piece of software couldn't do.)

- Do this 2-3x a day, during the hours of 5:00p.m. — 10:00p.m. EST.

And before you freak out I'm asking you to give

up your late-night viewings of "Castle" — just remember each of these "following sessions" should take only 2-3 minutes a piece. (Four minutes if you've already had that second glass of wine.)

And trust me, those four-minute flurries of following, commenting and liking, not only will help you avoid the Instagram spam police and build up your follower counts exponentially…

…but you'll also create some serious Instagram goodwill you can convert later on for some hard currency.

Instagram Tribe Buildin' Tip #4: @Mention and Spotlight Your Existing Followers

Once you've got a fairly decent collection of followers, and if you follow Tip #3 you'll have that before you know it, then you'll want to use three of my favorite strategies for boosting engagement with your existing followers:

1. @Mention followers in your Instagram posts (You do this by adding their @username in a post caption)

2. Share a follower's image in your own feed (You can do this by taking a screen shot with your phone and then cropping and uploading to your own feed. Be sure to ask permission FIRST!)

3. Share a follower's post on one of your other social media channels (Facebook, Pinterest and Twitter are ideal for this. Be sure to ask permission FIRST!)

And why would we want to embark on this bit of altruistic spelunking? Because this follower will pay it forward, by sharing your post with your inner circle. (Which will get you a new swath of followers and possible customers.)

Trust me: This is effective. But ya gotta schedule it, just like them following sessions. (Otherwise you'll never get around to it.)

Instagram Tribe Buildin' Tip #5: @Mention Celebs and Influencers

This is like the previous tip, only this time the person you are "mentioning" has the last name of Kardashian. (Or is a big influencer within your industry.)

And just like in the previous step, all you have to do is add the @username of the person you're trying to reach in your post caption.

Now you don't want to be a spammy jerk. Don't just add people for the sake of getting access to their followers. (It's not cool, and it frankly doesn't work.)

But if you have a genuine response to something a fellow Instagram user has said or created — let's say you've been moved by a book somebody wrote, or you think the influencer or celeb might be interested in your post...

...then knock yourself out. (Just don't lose sleep waiting for Katy Perry to get back to you.)

Instagram Tribe Buildin' Tip #6: Add a QR Code for In-Store Users

So, I have to be honest: I know next to nothing about how QR codes work. But apparently there is this witchcraft that lets you generate magical code...

...which you put in your place of business. (And which allows customers to scan with their phones and instantly lets them become a follower of your Instagram tribe.)

Like I said, I'm a real QR expert.

But, having worked with enough clients who have physical stores, I can tell you the Instagram QR strategy works (especially if your clientele is under 40)...

...as long as you give them an incentive to actually follow you. Just being added ain't enough. (Ya gotta do better than that.)

So, here's what I recommend:

- Create your QR code — Through whatever wizard means you do that)

- Create a compelling incentive — Follow us on Instagram to get 10% off your order or Follow us to be entered into a contest to go on a date with Natalie Portman (if only)
- Print out the QR code (or conjure it) and put it next to your register — Your clientele will see it

Wait? Contest? What's this about a contest? How do I do an Instagram contest?

So, glad you asked...

Instagram Tribe Buildin' Tip #7: Run a Frickin' Instagram Contest

This is more of an advanced tribe-buildin' tip, and one I wouldn't jump into until you've got at least 1000 followers. (Otherwise you won't see serious gains.)

But once you've got those 1K followers, I highly recommend you try it. (I schedule at least one contest every three months and always see a huge boost in LEADS and SALES.)

So, how do you run an Instagram contest? Here's the four-step process I follow each time:

1. Choose a non-sucky prize. Gift cards work great. (Especially if you're a brick-and-mortar shop or an e-commerce site) If you're a service business, then some kind of consultation or value service is a great prize.

2. Announce the rules of the contest in an Instagram post. It'll be some action that requires followers to a) Upload a photo of them expressing themselves or using your product and b) Using a pre-designated contest hashtag

3. Keep an eye on the hashtag. It's important you choose a unique hashtag. #SummerFun might sound like a great way to describe your contest, but it'll be a nightmare figuring out who actually entered the contest. (I generally go with something like #CompanyNameSpringContest…or

something like that.)

4. Announce the winner. You can do this either through a specific Instagram post or direct message to the winner yourself. (Or both.)

Like I said, su-per simple.

Once you get the hang of running a contest or two, you can try out different variations, such as:

-   Have people comment, like or share to enter a contest
-   Have people VOTE on an item of yours (with the winning item going on sale at deep discount)
-   Have people tag their friends (Example: "Tag a friend who is into the 'smoky eye' look...") — This type of contest is so popular it's got a dedicated hashtag — #TagAFriend
-   Any other fun and visually interesting (though legal) activity you can dream up to

have your followers do

There's no limit to the weird and wonderful ways you can use a contest to build your tribe (and put money in your pocket.)

Just don't have them watch one of those awful "Twilight" movies. (No prize is worth that.)

Chapter Six Key Takeaways:

- **It's simple, the more you post the more followers you get.** Recent content will always be king.

- **Gather new Instagram followers by simply asking for them on your website.** Generate "follow me on Instagram" code and place it in key areas such as your site's "About Me" page, sidebar and the footer of blog posts. (But don't forget about other places such as email signatures and Twitter bios.)

- **The most effective form of tribe-buildin' is to like, follow and comment on Instagram users.** Schedule 2-3x minute-long sessions where you like, comment and follow folks who represent the demographics of your ideal customer.

- **Boost your follower count by spotlighting your followers and fans.** Just mention their @username in a post and you'll not only get their engagement on a post — but most likely they'll share it with their own tribe.

- **You can also ping celebs and influencers with the same @username method.** The key is not to be too spammy — or too stalkerish because Taylor Swift didn't get right back to ya.

- **Though the author knows nothing about the witchcraft that is QR codes, he knows it works.** Just make sure you give people an incentive to follow you on Instagram.

- **Instagram contests work super frickin' well.** Choose a unique hashtag and a prize that doesn't suck. (Gift cards and one-on-one coaching sessions work best.)

Chapter 7:

Five Ninja-Hack Tools & Apps That Will Make You Money

"The best investment is in the tools of one's trade."
-Benjamin Franklin

We've come to my FAVORITE part of this book! (And it should be your favorite too.)

That's because I'm about to share with you my favorite ninja-hack apps and tools that'll not only save you a crap load of time...

…but also make you a crap load of money.

Now, some of these apps/tools are more on the advanced side. (For example, I don't recommend you jump right out and run an Instagram contest with Wishpond your first week out.)

But if you add these slowly, over the course of the next few weeks, you'll be shocked how quickly your Instagram efforts will start to pay off.

Quick word of warning: many of these apps have the lasting power of an NBC sitcom. (Not much.)

For instance, one of my FAVORITE tools ever — Iconosquare — was FREE for years. (Until they started charging $200/month. Yikes!)

So, do your due diligence before signing up for any of these apps/tools recommended below.

Okay, let's jump into the deep end of the Instagram app pool:

Instagram Ninja-Hack Tool #1: HootSuite (Instagram Post Scheduling Tool)

Posting on Instagram with your smartphone or tablet of choice has three major drawbacks:

- It's tough to type out lengthy captions without making a typo (or inducing carpal tunnel in your hands)
- Copying and pasting 15-20 relevant hashtags into a post is a nightmare
- Posting consistently during optimal Instagram times can be as difficult as 12th-grade pre-calculus

But worry not, Instagrammers, we have our champion! And that is the social media management tool, HootSuite.

HootSuite is a web/mobile app that lets you manage nearly ALL of your social media activity — I use it to churn out all my LinkedIn, Facebook,

Instagram and Twitter activity — in one simple, convenient location.

Best of all, it's FREE. (Though they have paid options, if you want more user accounts and broader analytics.)

Now HootSuite isn't PERFECT. (You can schedule posts for anytime — but in order to "publish" you have to "approve" a mobile notification for the post RIGHT before your scheduled publish time.)

And it doesn't work well when you repost other people's stuff (more on that next.)

But for a FREE tool that lets you do MOST of your Instagram activity right on your computer, it's a DAMN good addition to your overall Instagram marketing plan.

Instagram Ninja-Hack Tool #2: Repost for Instagram

HootSuite works great for posting original

Instagram content you create. But what about reposting other people's stuff? (Which is one of the most effective ways to get your profile noticed…notice other people first!)

That's where the Repost for Instagram app comes in.

Forget spending HOURS each week finding content you can repost and share with your followers. With this app you can scour Instagram, using keywords, to find users who might make for ideal prospects. (Lets you schedule a week's worth of Instagram content in just a few minutes.)

Here's how it works:

- Download the Repost for Instagram app
- Fire up the Instagram app
- Use keywords to find users who have interesting content AND who you'd like expose to your brand
- Click on one of their posts and then click on the three dots in the upper right
- Select "copy link"

- Open up your "Repost" app (the app will automatically recognize the post you copied a link for)
- Then when you WANT to…open the Repost app and publish the repost

Now it doesn't give you the ability to schedule posts. But it lets you create a reservoir of content, in just minutes, that you can then go back and publish when you need to fill your quota. (I recommend 5pm and 10pm EST Tuesday -Thursday, at the least.)

This may not pay huge dividends right away. But if you stick with it, you'll slowly build a legion of Instagram followers.

And then you'll be ready for…

Instagram Ninja-Hack Tool #3: Follow Liker

The FollowLiker app is so powerful I almost don't want to tell you about it.

It's that good.

But if you want to build your follower numbers up to 2-3k, in a matter of weeks, you must:

- Follow a ton of people in your target audience
- Like posts by your target audience
- Unfollow folks who didn't follow you back
- Keep doing it for hours and hours each week until your finger bleed

And if that sounds fun, and if enjoy getting your teeth drilled, then don't let me stand in your way. But if you'd like to skip all the manual work, and let automation take over, then Follow Liker is a great way to go.

Here's how it works:

- **Purchase FollowLiker.** Yep. Sorry. It's not FREE. But at $75 it's worth it.
- **Find a computer you use little.** That old laptop you spilled coffee on will work.
- **Set parameters to the software.** (More on that soon.) And let it do it's thing in the

background.

- **Watch as your follower count climbs**.

Before you freak out that a tool that does things like mass following, liking and unfollowing will get you exiled to the Instagram prison colony, just know with the conservative settings below you'll ensure you don't risk censure from the Insta-Police.

When setting up your FollowLiker account you'll want to:

- **Skip one day off a week.** Using this tool 24/7 is a great way to get your account banned.
- **Operate only during the day.** Or at night. But not both.
- **Impose daily limits.** I like to limit the tool to only 100-150 follows per day, only 100 unfollows per day, and only 200 likes of individual photos per day. Stick with those and stay well within bounds.
- **Insert a 60-second delay between**

actions. You don't want the tool just going non-stop. You want it to appear organic. And adding a one-minute delay will do that.

Instagram Ninja-Hack Tool #4: A Second Instagram Account (For Super-Sneaky Hyperlinks)

This is my FAVORITE ninja-hack on the entire list. Mostly because it's really effective and NOBODY else uses it. (Except for me and my crazy clients.)

But here's the basic concept:

- Instagram DOESN'T allow LINKS in the captions of your Instagram posts - The only external link you can have is right below your bio
- Instagram DOES allow you to link to other Instagram accounts - by simply adding @username in the caption of the post
- So, what we do is create a SECOND

Instagram account (such as @mybusinessfreebie) and add that to our caption

- And when users click over to that 2nd Instagram account they see our promotional goodness (and we get around the NO LINK Instagram caption rule)

I know this may sound like a lot of work. All you're doing is creating a dedicated SECOND Instagram account and then creating 3-4 Instagram posts (with great images and strong text call-outs) that promote that all-important special offer or freebie giveaway you're hawking.

Because here's the funny thing: you'd think research would show that these extra "hoops" you're making people run through would be bad for conversions. (Actually the opposite is true.)

The more you keep asking people for "small" commitments, but still keep them in their "native" Instagram environment, the more likely they'll take a positive action you want when they finally reach your landing page.

Now, again your offer needs to be good. It needs to be a great discount or freebie giveaway…or amazing offer that nobody can resist. (Don't just hawk expensive crap nobody wants.)

But the cool thing is you can create as many of these PROMO Instagram accounts as you want. (Maybe one for each of your products and services.)

So, give this technique a try. (Just promise not to share it with everybody you know. We gotta hold on to our competitive advantages as long as we can.)

Instagram Ninja-Hack Tool #5: WishPond (Instagram Contest App)

So, as we went over in the last chapter, Instagram contests are a fantastic way to build your Instagram following. (And even turn those followers into warm leads.)

But some logical, tech-y contest stuff can be a pain to deal with. That's why I recommend a contest tool, such as WishPond.

Basically what WishPond does is offer you:

- **Templates for creating mobile-responsive contest landing pages** (that you can then publish on your website, Facebook page or Twitter stream super EASILY)

- **And then they handle the collection of all the leads.** (My favorite type of contest is the Instagram hashtag contest — and the awesome thing is WishPond will collect all the photos…so you don't have to sift through them.)

- **Most importantly: WishPond takes care of all the contest terms of service and regulations.** (This can be a pain and they make sure you totally comply with Instagram's rules of the contest road.)

Now, WishPond has a ton of different payment options, depending on how many leads you acquire (and how many internal users you need.) But they have a 14-day trial I highly recommend you check out. (Even if just to try out your FIRST contest.)

Chapter Seven Key Takeaways:

- **HootSuite is a fantastic FREE tool that lets you create and schedule your Instagram posts ahead of time.** You will have to "approve" each scheduled post on your mobile device, but this FREE tool will save you a crap load of time.

- **The Repost for Instagram app is a marvelous way to gather content** to fill your Instagram coffers in just a couple minutes a week.

- **FollowLiker is a great tool for automating the liking and following of folks in your target audience.** Be sure to use the limits outlined above to avoid a crackdown from the Instagram police.

- **A second Instagram account is the ideal super-ninja way to get around the "can't link in Instagram posts" rule.** Just create a dedicated second account, for a particular offer or product, and then fill that account with posts that direct users to your location of choice.

- **WishPond is the perfect Instagram contest tool.** They let you create mobile-friendly contest landing pages and handle all the lead collection and hashtag monitoring for you. (Big time-saver!)

Epilogue: "Toto, I Don't Think We're in Kansas Anymore"

I wish I could tell you Instagram was just a blip on the marketing radar screen.

That its practitioners' obsession with hashtags and selfies and sepia-toned pictures of…God knows what…is just a slight deviation from an otherwise straight trajectory toward a more nuanced and refined society.

But you and I both know that just ain't the case.

Things are only gonna get more vain, more narcissistic, and more superficial — future academics will call it the "Kardashian factor" — and Instagram is the ultimate reflection of a generation absolutely consumed with presenting themselves in the most hip and attractive way. (So they can be validated with a flurry of likes, comments and follows.)

But having plumbed these Instagram depths for the last year I can tell you that underneath the shallow Instagram posts and the inappropriate and stupefyingly inane comments is something far darker and more profound...

...a need to be seen. (And heard. And understood.)

And if you're able to offer your message (and your products) not in some antiquated 50s sales-y way...

...but as an opportunity for young people to get noticed in a world that's as distracted as a four-year-old on Red Bull...

...then you'll not just sell more stuff. (Which is always nice.) But you'll create an army of loyal (and socially connected) users who can spread your company's message faster and far more cheaply than you ever could. (Even with 30 seconds during the Super Bowl.)

So, look past all the pouty-lip selfies and the six-pack ab mirror pictures and just ask yourself…how can my product or service make my tribe look smarter/hipper/more attractive/morally superior than their friends?

If you're able to do that, then your business will have more momentum than a four-year-old on Red Bull.

Good luck with your Instagram marketing!

And if you've enjoyed this book, or even if you didn't enjoy the book, would you be willing to leave a review?

Even a sentence or two really helps us indie authors carve out a career as a creative professional.

Head over to PunkRockMarketing.com/Instabook to leave a review on Amazon (and enjoy truckloads of good

karma):

Oh, and just one more thing...

A Special FREE Gift for You!

If you'd like FREE instant access to my seminar "How to Make a Damn Good Living With Social Media (Even If You Hate Social Media" then head over to **PunkRockMarketing.com/Free**. (What else you gonna do? Watch another "Twilight" movie?!)

DISCLAIMER AND/OR LEGAL NOTICES:

Every effort has been made to accurately represent this book and it's potential. Results vary with every individual, and your results may or may not be different from those depicted. No promises, guarantees or warranties, whether stated or implied, have been made that you will produce any specific result from this book. Your efforts are individual and unique, and may vary from those shown. Your success depends on your efforts, background and motivation.

The material in this publication is provided for educational and informational purposes only and is not intended as business advice. Use of the programs, advice, and information contained in this book is at the sole choice and risk of the reader.

Made in the USA
Middletown, DE
14 February 2019